VICTORIAN AND EDWARDIAN RAILWAY TRAVEL

David Turner

SHIRE PUBLICATIONS

Published in Great Britain in 2013 by Shire Publications Ltd, Midland House, West Way, Botley, Oxford OX2 0PH, United Kingdom.

43-01 21st Street, Suite 220B, Long Island City, NY 11101, USA.

E-mail: shire@shirebooks.co.uk   www.shirebooks.co.uk

A CIP catalogue record for this book is available from the British Library.

Shire Library no. 689.   ISBN-13: 978 0 74781 150 3

David Turner has asserted his right under the Copyright, Designs and Patents Act, 1988, to be identified as the author of this book.

Designed by Tony Truscott Designs, Sussex, UK and typeset in Perpetua and Gill Sans.

Printed in China through Worldprint Ltd.

13 14 15 16 17   10 9 8 7 6 5 4 3 2 1

COVER IMAGE
The Travelling Companions, painted in 1862 by Augustus Leopold Egg, depicted the height of luxury for first class travellers in the 1860s; including an enclosed carriage, soft furnishings and window blinds. However, the smoothness of the ride in the period was still not always assured. Though the scene depicted is in France, the travelling experience in Britain was much the same at the time.

TITLE PAGE IMAGE
The last broad-gauge train passing through Sonning Cutting on 20 May 1892.

CONTENTS PAGE IMAGE
Passengers wait for trains at Woolston Station on the London and South Western Railway in the 1890s.

ACKNOWLEDGEMENTS
Illustrations are acknowledged as follows:

Birmingham Museums and Art Gallery/The Bridgeman Art Library, cover image; Jo Edkins Collection, page 13; John Collection, 46 (top); Lens of Sutton, page 9 (middle Look and Learn/The Bridgeman Art Library, page 32; National Railway Museum, York/The Bridgeman Art Library, page 26 (bottom); Science and Society Picture Library, pages 1, 5, 10, 11 (bottom), 13 (top), 20, 22, 24, 26 (top), 27 (top), 31 (top and bottom), 34 (bottom), 40, 41, 44, 49, 50 (bottom).
All other images are from the author's collection.

Shire Publications is supporting the Woodland Trust, the UK's leading woodland conservation charity, by funding the dedication of trees.

CONTENTS

INTRODUCTION

O<small>N</small> 27 September 1825 six hundred people travelled on the first train on the Stockton & Darlington Railway (SDR). This was a landmark event. Before 1825 most tramways were constructed for the purpose of transporting minerals, and the vast majority were operated by horses. The SDR's promoters, too, expected that its traffic would be principally freight, and when the other pioneering railway of the age, the Liverpool & Manchester Railway (LMR), opened in 1830, the belief was still that goods traffic would dominate.

Yet they were wrong. The LMR carried on average 1,100 passengers daily until 1833, and when new lines appeared passenger traffic continued to dominate. Consequently, while in 1842 Britain's many railway companies earned £1.6 million from freight, they carried 24.5 million passengers earning them £3.1 million. Not until the 1850s did goods revenue exceed that from passengers. Passengers always remained important for the railways business, and in 1900 1.1 billion passengers generated £38 million, or 38 per cent of the industry's revenue.

London Bridge station was one of the busiest in the Victorian period, as shown by this scene of the station's crowds in 1858.

The experience of railway travel changed dramatically over the Victorian period. In 1825, passengers had to clamber into wagons from ground level, were exposed to the elements in open carriages, and were moved slowly by modern standards. Seventy-five years later, they departed from stations that had refreshment rooms, waiting rooms, ticket offices, newspaper stands and toilets. They could buy different classes of ticket, were conveyed safely at over 90 miles per hour and in carriages up to 50 feet long, which could have dining, sleeping and toilet facilities. Furthermore, accident insurance for journeys could be purchased, passengers could have their luggage sent on ahead of them, and they could travel to hundreds of destinations for work or pleasure.

However, while the changes in passengers' experience were dramatic, at no point could they be labelled revolutionary. Rather, railway travel evolved over time through trial and error on the companies' part, through passengers complaining about the services they received, and, regrettably, through accidents that highlighted the need for safety improvements. While the basic features of railway passenger services were established before 1870, developments thereafter helped to evolve the modern experience of railway travel. This book charts those changes.

By the end of the Victorian period, the majority of the population used railways to travel, there being little alternative for most journeys. This is Bexhill Station on the South Eastern and Chatham Railway in 1905.

THE STATION EXPERIENCE

THE MODERN CONCEPTION of a railway station did not exist in 1825, and the SDR's first passengers clambered into the wagons from the ground, but railway companies quickly found it necessary to provide travellers with accommodation, although some of their attempts were poor. The SDR soon converted a warehouse at Darlington; the Leeds & Selby Railway's stations from 1834 had no platforms, and tickets were purchased at the superintendent's house; Hartlepool station in 1840 was the poop of an old Dutch cargo boat. Furthermore, some railway companies, like the stagecoach operators, sold tickets in public houses. These makeshift facilities existed because of the industry's emergent nature and, occasionally, the companies' poor financial state.

The LMR constructed the first purpose-built stations at Liverpool Road in Manchester and at Crown Street, Liverpool. Resembling classical town houses, they established the station arrangement that has endured until the modern day. There were offices where tickets and information could be obtained, waiting rooms, canopies, and platforms accessible only through the station building. The only unfamiliar feature was that they had a single platform for both arrivals and departures, something which for a short time was the norm everywhere. Only on the Great Western Railway (GWR) were passengers afforded two platforms from the outset. However, as traffic increased in the 1830s, companies began building two platforms, one each for 'up' and 'down' trains at through stations, with separate arrival and departure platforms at termini.

However, another change was occurring, and from the 1850s larger stations started becoming architectural masterpieces. Norwich, York, St Pancras, King's Cross, Birmingham Curzon Street and Bristol were majestic temples of the railway age, combining beauty with functionality. Yet by the late 1860s rising passenger numbers forced railways to rebuild their largest stations to increase capacity. Birmingham Snow Hill was rebuilt in 1871 and 1912, as was Crewe in 1867 and between 1896 and 1906. Glasgow Central was rebuilt in two stages in 1879 and between 1901

Opposite:
The artistic skill of the railway engineer reached its height with the construction of the Midland Railway's St Pancras station in the 1860s. This photograph of brickwork and ironwork in the main trainshed shows some of the finer details.

On the Liverpool & Manchester Railway, as elsewhere, intermediate stations were basic structures with little in the way of amenities.

and 1906. Waterloo was completely rebuilt between 1900 and 1922 Furthermore, other large termini were extended and widened. These work caused problems for railway managers, who had to maintain services whil construction was in progress.

While large stations were of a generally good standard, local one varied in quality, and especially before the 1880s, for cost reasons companies resisted making improvements until they were essential An assessment of the London & North Western's (LNWR) Huyton Quarr station in 1867 was that it belonged 'to some bankrupt company, who coul not afford a few pounds to put it in a tolerably decent condition'. In 188(*Punch* commented that the London & South Western Railway's (LSWR 'directors must be great rabbit fanciers, for the number of hutches scattere over their "system" is enormous'. However, 'these hutches are not fo rabbits, but for humans, and … they are technically known as "Countr Stations".' Indeed, although most companies directed staff to kee stations clean, the idyllic image of the British country station was actuall a product of the early twentieth century. Nevertheless, the opulence o the large stations could be found replicated at more humble locations William Tite designed Hampton Court station in a Tudor style to matc the palace it served.

Ancillary services appeared at stations early in the railway age. The first wer news stands and bookstalls. Initially, the vendors were railwaymen's widow or crippled ex-employees who sold soiled newspapers, 'improper literature

Newark station on the Great Northern Railway in 1910.

Hampton Court station, shown in 1905, was designed by William Tite and opened in 1849.

Birmingham New Street station, opened in 1854 by the London & North Western and Midland railways, was one of many impressive feats of station engineering.

and poor-quality refreshments. However, in August 1848 William Smith who had an established national network of newspaper sellers, approached the LNWR with a proposal, which it accepted. For £1,500 he obtained contract to sell newspapers at the company's stations, the first bookstall opening at Euston on 1 November 1848. By 1865 contracts had been secured with most British railway companies, and W. H. Smith's monopoly on newspaper selling was secure until around 1900.

Refreshment rooms for passengers also appeared early on, possibly the first appearing at the Grand Junction Railway's Birmingham terminus in 1837. They soon became commonplace, with larger stations usually having separate refreshment rooms for the different classes of passenger. As they do today, they served customers starting journeys or changing trains, but they were also used by those on long-distance trains, which would stop at some stations for about ten to twenty minutes to enable refreshments to be taken. Indeed, at Nuneaton station one could purchase a six-course meal for 2s 6d. However, with dining cars being increasingly introduced on long-distance routes from the 1880s, these stops were phased out on many such services.

By 1900 W. H. Smith dominated the newspaper and bookselling market at stations. This is the company's news stand at Marylebone station, London, in 1905.

Throughout the period refreshment rooms were notorious for the poor quality of their food. In 1867 Charles Dickens's publication *All the Year Round* described 'The pork and veal pies, with their bumps of delusive promise and their little cubes of gristle and bad fat … the sawdusty sandwiches, so frequently and energetically condemned.' The service was also questionable: 'the icy stare from the counter, the insolent ignoring of every customer's existence, which drives the hungry frantic, all these are doomed.' Nevertheless, some refreshment-room services became more professional, and those taken over by the contractors Spiers & Pond were of particular note for their high quality. Yet complaints remained, and in 1892 the *Leicester Chronicle* printed the following:

Railway companies not only owned refreshment rooms, they also produced their own cutlery and crockery for them. This is a Great Northern Railway cream jug from the 1890s.

While refreshment rooms around the railway network were of varying quality, those at termini were usually well kept. This shows the Paddington station refreshment room in 1923.

Facilities available to passengers at Waterloo station, c. 1900.

Throughout the Victorian period railway companies handed out their own timetables, and this example from the London & North Western Railway of 1869 is typical.

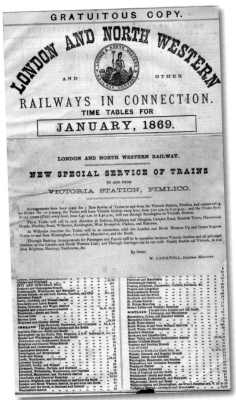

GRATUITOUS COPY.

LONDON AND NORTH WESTERN

AND OTHER

RAILWAYS IN CONNECTION.

TIME TABLES FOR

JANUARY, 1869.

LONDON AND NORTH WESTERN RAILWAY.

NEW SPECIAL SERVICE OF TRAINS
TO AND FROM
VICTORIA STATION, PIMLICO.

Traveller: 'My friend, there's no meat in this sandwich.'

Waitress: 'No?'

Traveller: 'Don't you think you'd better give that pack another shuffle and let me draw again?'

Another common feature of stations from the 1840s was the lavatory. At smaller stations toilets could be simple, and at the Midland Railway's Weston station passengers used the toilet in the stationmaster's house until 1894. Toilets at larger stations were better, and towards the end of the century they could be luxuriously equipped with bathrooms and hairdressing salons.

Other services found at larger stations after 1870 included fruit and flower stalls, bootblacks, and sweet and tobacco kiosks, and just before 1914 some even had post offices and chemists.

Railway operations were necessarily of a regimented nature and this was well reflected in the companies' timetables. The LMR published the first, named a 'scheme of departures', in 1830, and throughout the

entury all companies produced their own, which, in addition to train
imes, included sample fares, their arrangements for sending luggage,
egal notices, and advertisements for their services.

However, the most famous compendium of railway timetables in the
'ictorian period was *Bradshaw*. In 1838 George Bradshaw, a Manchester
rinter, published a booklet containing all the railway timetables he could
btain. By 1842 this had evolved into the *Bradshaw's Monthly Railway Guides*,
letailing all train services in Britain and Ireland. Because of its comprehensive
ature it became a household name. For example, in the Sherlock Holmes
tory *The Adventure of the Copper Beeches*, Dr Watson discovered that there
vas '"a train at half-past nine", said I, glancing over my *Bradshaw*. "It is due
t Winchester at 11.30".' Nevertheless, many found the vast amount of
nformation it contained overwhelming. In 1869 Anthony Trollope wrote
f his uncertainty regarding when he would arrive in Glasgow: 'I cannot learn
vithout an amount of continued study of *Bradshaw* for which I have neither the
trength nor mental ability.'

From 1853 the main competitor was the *ABC Guides*, which listed services
o and from London. Their unique selling point was that they provided

Bradshaw's Railway Guide was the archetypal timetable of the age. This is a page from the 1843 edition showing trains to and from Manchester.

LONDON. AUGUST, 1907.

GREAT CENTRAL RAILWAY OFFICIAL

MONTHLY ½D

ABC

FORWARD

TIME-TABLE INCLUDING

AN ORIGINAL

TALE TOLD IN THE TRAIN

RAPID TRAVEL IN LUXURY

FIRST CLASS

The **TATLER** with illustrated Sporting and Country House Supplement.

6ᴰ. WEEKLY.

Buy The **TATLER** To enjoy Travelling

The main competitor to *Bradshaw* was the *ABC Guide*. This edition, detailing Great Central Railway services, also contained a 'Tale Told in the Train' for the traveller's entertainment.

The Edmondson ticket became the standard design used by Britain's railways, surviving until 1990.

information on fares. They were successful even if they could not tell travellers how to get from Bath to Glasgow. For a short time Bradshaw attempted to compete by also providing details of fares. Yet, with the number of services increasing nationally, space in his guides became limited and this was abandoned. Nonetheless, the three timetable types, the companies' own, *Bradshaw* and the *ABC Guide*, coexisted until after the First World War.

Having discovered the time of his or her train, the passenger required a ticket indicating that he or she had paid the fare permitting travel. Early tickets varied in nature. As with stagecoaches, some were prebooked, with passengers receiving waybills torn from a counterfoil book. Other companies used handwritten tickets, while the London & Greenwich Railway used reusable metal tokens.

A major innovation came in 1836 when Thomas Edmondson, a Newcastle & Carlisle Railway stationmaster, developed a new ticket system to address the fact that existing systems were losing companies revenue through fare evasion. His system used small preprinted cards for different journeys, which were serially numbered by hand. Soon after, the date and serial numbers were applied by a machine automatically. The Edmondson ticket was such a success that in 1842 the Railway Clearing House, an organisation established to co-ordinate the allocation of revenue between railway companies, introduced them nationwide. They remained in use until February 1990.

Nevertheless, fare evasion remained a problem for the railways. In 1858 a Midland Railway ticket inspector, Mr Draycott, reported at a trial that 'attempts were made daily to defraud railway companies'. Indeed, in 1914, when an engineer earning £1,200 per year was in court for the crime, the judge said that 'it was quite bad enough when they ad the poorest of the poor doing this sort of thing', suggesting that it was frequent occurrence.

Passengers, especially those not returning the same day, would often e accompanied by luggage. Apart from speed of travel, the efficient movement of luggage was a major advantage the railways had over tagecoaches. Generally, luggage was left in cloakrooms when passengers rrived at stations. It was then labelled by staff, who loaded it on to the rain. In the 1830s, 1840s and 1850s it was usually carried on carriage roofs. Iowever, sparks from locomotives caused fires, and the practice was phased ut. From the 1860s luggage was placed in guards' vans with the guard, vho had responsibility for unloading it at the correct station. To avoid being tranded without luggage, passengers could also send it ahead several days efore their journey.

How much luggage a person could send quickly became established. rom 1830 the LMR allowed passengers to transport 60 pounds of luggage vithout charge. Yet it was soon loosely established by railway companies that irst-class passengers could carry 150 pounds free, second-class 120 pounds, nd third-class 100 pounds. However, what constituted 'luggage' varied etween 1830 and 1900. In 1869 children's rocking horses were not deemed o be luggage, but in 1873 sewing machines were. Debates of this nature vent on throughout the period, with some cases going to court.

Aspects of the station experience, including the layout, refreshment ooms, bookstalls, tickets, luggage practices and timetables, were all stablished before the 1860s and refined thereafter. Furthermore, railway ompanies offered new services after the 1870s, and by 1900 stations had volved into the form familiar to us today.

Labels such as these were the main means by which the railways were able to route luggage from one station to another.

Having to convey a large volume of luggage, railway companies from an early date built dedicated luggage vans, such as this example from the South Eastern & Chatham Railway.

THE TRAIN

THE HISTORY of railway carriage development cannot be written by simply examining a single company's contributions to their designs. The advances should always be framed by the political, cultural and economic factors that propelled change.

Most of the Stockton & Darlington's carriages in 1825 were open trucks, in line with the management's intent to convey mainly goods. Yet its first train did possess Britain's first covered railway carriage. Nicknamed 'Experiment', it was a truck modified with a coach body, doors at each end, windows, soft furnishings and a table. It was reserved for higher-paying customers, so it also represented the first appearance of class distinctions in railway travel.

Existing modes of transport, such as stagecoaches and steamboats, provided only two classes. But the railways' greater speed and regularity allowed companies to offer a broader range of services to different customers. Indeed, while most early railways had two classes of accommodation, by the late 1830s three was the norm. First-class passengers had the best carriages, which were furnished, glazed and covered. Second-class accommodation had roofs and acceptable seats but was usually open to the elements on either side, while third-class passengers travelled in what were little better than open trucks with wooden seats. In 1838 the *Sheffield Independent* described these as being 'of common appearance but substantial in structure, and being open will probably be preferred in fine weather'. Yet by the 1860s, on most railways, both second- and third-class accommodation had become fully enclosed, even if their internal fittings remained relatively unchanged.

Before the 1860s most railway companies attached third-class carriages only to early-morning or goods trains, because first- and second-class traffic was more profitable. In the year ending June 1846, 53 per cent of Britain's 23 million railway passengers travelled first or second class, generating 76 per cent of the industry's £4.7 million of passenger revenue. For the companies, accommodating higher volumes of third-class traffic would force

Opposite:
This image
from an edition
of *British Workmen*
shows the
cramped
conditions within
carriages in
the 1860s.

Early carriages, such as these first-class examples from the Liverpool & Manchester Railway, were little more than stagecoaches on railway axles.

[Locomotive Engine, and part of a train of first-class Carriages.]

up costs and lower profits. Furthermore, even third-class travel was out o many people's price range before 1870. Consequently third-class trave received little promotion, and advertisements on the opening of the LSWR Hampton Court branch in 1849 did not mention such tickets being available

Nevertheless, because of the poor quality of third-class accommodatior it was the first to be significantly improved, and the first major governmen legislation regarding the railways concerned how poorer passengers travellec On Christmas Eve 1841 a GWR goods train from Bristol to London wa passing through Sonning Cutting, east of Reading. In the train third-clas passengers were travelling in open coaches, positioned between th locomotive and the goods wagons. Heavy rains had caused a landslip, and o hitting it the train derailed, causing the third-class coaches to be crushec Eight people died at the scene, and another the day after, and sixteen wer seriously injured. The Board of Trade's report stated that a lack of protectio for the passengers was the principal cause of the deaths.

Consequently, the Board of Trade began an enquiry into third-clas accommodation, culminating in the 1844 Regulation of Railways Act This compelled railway companies deriving at least a third of their revenu

While early carriages were basic, many had striking liveries. This image of a Liverpool & Manchester Railway first-class carriage from 1838 shows the way in which early carriages were painted.

from passengers to provide one cheap train daily on each route for poorer individuals. Importantly, the railways had to use enclosed carriages with seats. These were nicknamed 'Parliamentary Trains' or 'Parlies'. However, the 'Parly' became a separate class of train, and open carriages remained in service until the early 1870s.

Overall, before 1870 passenger traffic was steadily increasing, and so there was no pressure on the companies to improve their carriage designs drastically, apart from a gradual disappearance of open carriages and the covering of third-class accommodation. An LSWR second-class carriage of the mid-1840s was 15 feet long, while its 1862 successor was 21 feet. Indeed, by 1870 Britain's longest carriages were only around 27 feet in length. There had been some improvements, including sprung buffers and oil lighting, yet poor ride comfort and cramped compartments persisted.

Railway carriages developed greatly between 1837 and 1900, as this postcard from 1904 shows.

After 1870 massive passenger traffic growth and a change in the public's expectation of rail travel forced companies to improve their carriage accommodation. In 1870 Britain's railways conveyed 330 million passengers. By 1885 the total was 697 million, and in 1899 the figure was 1,107 million. The growth is attributable to increased third-class traffic across the period. In 1870 it constituted 67 per cent of all passengers conveyed. However, by 1899 the proportion was 91 per cent. Furthermore, the proportion of individuals travelling second class declined considerably. In 1870, 22.2 per cent of all passengers travelled by second class, while by 1899 the proportion was only 6.0 per cent. One major factor was the numerous improvements in the quality and format of railway carriages for

This drawing-room carriage, built by the South Eastern & Chatham Railway after 1900, was the epitome of carriage technology before the First World War.

third-class travellers, and the Midland Railway was largely responsible for initiating these changes.

Because of its new lines to London in 1868 and between Settle and Carlisle in 1876, from the early 1870s the Midland reformed its passenger business to attract new customers. In 1872 it added third-class accommodation to all trains. In 1875 it was the first major company to abolish second-class accommodation, concurrently reducing first-class ticket prices and improving third-class compartments to old second-class standards. Lastly, on its new Settle to Carlisle route it introduced carriages that were twice as long as contemporary designs, containing both first- and third-class compartments. They also possessed improved ride comfort because at each end of the carriage two sets of wheels were held in swivelling bogies on bearings that absorbed the undulations in the track better than traditional fixed-wheel arrangements.

Initially these improvements caused anger and consternation from other companies, particularly the Midland's competitors. Yet, because of them the industry reassessed the quality of its passenger accommodation and pricing, as increasingly vocal passengers had had their expectations raised by the Midland's actions. From the 1870s other companies began attaching third-class accommodation to all trains, and by the late 1880s this was standard practice.

A Great Northern Railway East Coast express, c. 1906, showing long carriages on six-wheel bogies.

Additionally, bogie carriages slowly increased in number on long-distance routes. Some people, such as Patrick Stirling, Locomotive Superintendent of the Great Northern Railway (GNR), suggested that they had no future given their higher construction costs. Indeed, the GWR and LNWR were still building eight-wheeled non-bogie carriages for long-distance trains in the 1880s. Nevertheless, Stirling's predictions were wrong, and by 1900 longer bogie carriages were universally found on long-distance routes. Consequently, between 1870 and 1914 carriages became longer and heavier, and the total weight of some trains on the East Coast Main Line rose from 123 to 268 tons between 1870 and 1887.

Furthermore, on short-distance and suburban routes four-wheeled carriages were displaced by six-wheeled vehicles, which slightly improved ride comfort. These carriages persisted until the early twentieth century for the high-density traffic on suburban routes, because the cheaper and lighter six-wheeled carriages kept companies' costs lower, especially when third-class passengers, who generated less revenue per person, were increasing in number. Nevertheless, bogie carriages also began appearing on these routes around 1900.

Consequently, throughout the period most companies found it progressively uneconomical to provide second-class accommodation, as increasing numbers of passengers travelled in the improved third-class compartments at a cheaper cost. In many cases the removal of second-class accommodation in trains enhanced companies' profitability by reducing the costs of carriage construction and train marshalling. Thus, the GNR, the Manchester, Sheffield and Lincolnshire Railway (MSLR) and the Cheshire Lines Railway withdrew second class on long-distance services in the 1880s, and in the early 1890s the North Eastern (NER), Great Eastern (GER) and all Scottish railways abandoned it completely.

Indeed, with the GWR and LNWR dispensing with it on all trains in 1910 and 1912 respectively, two classes of passenger travel became the industry norm. Only the LSWR and the South Eastern & Chatham Railway (SECR) preserved second-class accommodation on main-line services after 1914, as they conveyed mainly passengers and second class remained profitable. Eventually, the LSWR removed it in 1918, and the SECR in 1923.

Initially, railways were significant because of their haulage capabilities. Yet the ability to carry passengers at speed soon became a prominent feature. Commenting on the SDR's opening, newspapers remarked that *Locomotion* could pull a greater load than four horses, and a carriage at a faster speed. But this was just the beginning, and thereafter advances in technology gradually increased train speeds.

On the Liverpool & Manchester's inaugural day, the speed of the trains was monitored carefully. Indeed, *Rocket* set the world record of 36 mph, conveying the mortally wounded William Huskisson (who had been run over) to Eccles. However, in the early period train speeds were infrequently measured, and speedometers were not uniformly fitted to locomotives until the twentieth century. Nevertheless, occasional records were taken. The GWR's locomotive *Ixion* averaged 54.6 mph between Paddington and

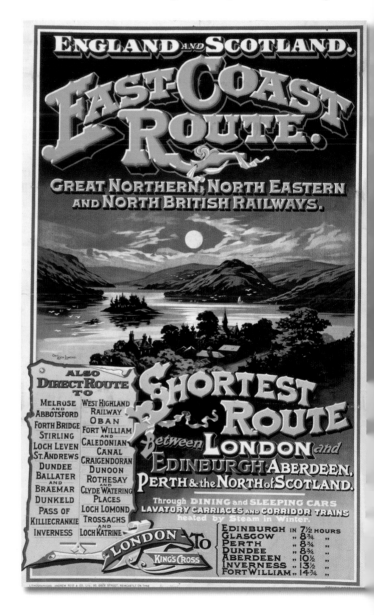

Both East and West Coast railway companies promoted their services heavily in the early 1900s. The Great Northern, North Eastern and North British Railways had to co-operate to provide a complete route to the north on the East Coast line.

Didcot in 1845. George Findlay stated that a fast train covered the 401 miles between London and Edinburgh in 1872 in nine hours ten minutes, including stoppages – an average speed of 43.7 mph.

Speeds got much greater during the 'Race to the North' in 1888 when the East Coast railway companies, the GNR, NER and the North British Railway (NBR), competed with the LNWR on the West Coast route to achieve the fastest service between London and Scotland. Technological improvements allowed the timetabled nine-hour journey on the East Coast route to be reduced to seven hours twenty-seven minutes, or an average of 53.8 mph, including a twenty-minute break for lunch at York. Many were impressed, and Lord Shaftesbury stated that year that his train 'spanked along the road to Liverpool. It is quite a just remark that the Devil, if he travelled, would go by train.'

Overnight races to Scotland began in 1895. On 20 August 1895 trains on the East Coast route achieved an average speed between London and Edinburgh of 63.5 mph. However, two days later the LNWR's locomotive *Hardwicke* covered the 141-mile stretch between Crewe and Carlisle at an average speed of 67.2 mph.

Ultimately, the races did not attract much more traffic to either route. Indeed, because carriage weights had increased as designs became larger, the races were uneconomical. Consequently, the East and West Coast companies eventually agreed that journey times between London and Edinburgh would go no lower than eight and a quarter hours. Nevertheless, the races improved the rapidity of regular services for passengers by raising performance benchmarks.

Most of the developments in carriage design occurred after 1870, but any economies the companies obtained from carriages' enlarged capacities were negated by the trains' higher speed and increased weight, as locomotives had to increase in power, raising their fuel consumption. Consequently, it has been suggested that the heavier trains of the period affected the industry's profitability. Despite this, the travelling experience for all passengers was much improved by 1900.

Hardwicke was the fastest locomotive in the 1895 'Race to the North', averaging 63.5 mph between Crewe and Carlisle. It is now part of the National Railway Museum's collection.

INSIDE THE CARRIAGE

WITHIN THE CONFINES of the carriage, individuals could do much more in 1900 than they could in 1830. Railway passengers in 1830 could do only what they could do in a stagecoach, for example watch the scenery go by, chat with fellow passengers, or read a book, light permitting. Yet by 1900 the experience of railway travel had become unique, and passengers could read in full illumination, smoke, dine in luxury, sleep and relieve themselves if necessary.

Initially, most railway companies prohibited smoking on their premises and trains, to prevent fire, and for the comfort of non-smokers. In 1831 the LMR restricted it in first-class accommodation, as the compartments had upholstery and fittings, and in 1838 it extended the ban to all services. Furthermore, most companies, such as the London & Birmingham Railway (LBR), GWR, LSWR and GER, prohibited smoking when they opened. The LSWR's 1845 rule book stated that

> Smoking is strictly prohibited both in the carriages, and in the company's stations. Every person smoking in a carriage or station is hereby subjected to a penalty not exceeding forty shillings.

These bans were formalised by the Railway Clauses Act of 1845, allowing companies to introduce by-laws to prevent the activity.

However, passengers flagrantly ignored these by-laws. In December 1855 the *Essex Standard* reported that Greenwich magistrates fined a passenger 10s for smoking on a London, Brighton & South Coast Railway (LBSCR) train. However, a third-class passenger wrote to *The Times* on the day of the case stating that in his carriage that day 'no less than five passengers were smoking'. Consequently, the LBSCR promised to crack down on offenders, as did the GWR in 1865.

Nevertheless smoking persisted, and in the 1860s some railways, such as the GER, GNR and LSWR, began accommodating smokers through providing 'smoking compartments'. Yet, not until the 1868 Regulation

Opposite:
Toilets installed in trains around 1900 were quite sophisticated, such as this LNWR example from 1906, which included a water closet, washbasin, hot and cold water supply and electric lighting.

A typical scene inside a second-class passenger compartment in the mid-1850s, painted by Abraham Solomon.

of Railways Act did these becom widespread, the act stating that

All Railway Companies ... shall, from and after the First Day of October next, in every Passenger Train where there are more carriages than one of each class, provide Smoking Compartments for each class of passengers...

Only the Metropolitan Railway wa exempted, because some of its servic was subterranean, but it too eventuall provided smoking accommodation in 1874.

While smoking compartments gradually became common, 'ladies only compartments did not. In the 1860s there was a surge in reports of assault on women travelling alone. In 1864 *The Standard* printed a letter fror a man whose servant had been in a compartment when three men spok rudely to her. She then stood by the window, but one man attempted t pull her to the floor and 'caught hold of her leg ... putting his hands u to her knee'. They then pushed her against the side of the carriage violent and alighted. Cases such as this put pressure on the railways to introduc dedicated compartments for women only. In October 1874 th Metropolitan Railway introduced them on all trains and was widely praise

However, the experiment failed miserably and the Metropolita abandoned the compartments soon after their introduction. The *York Heral*

Third-class accommodation was very frequently overloaded, as this painting by Solomon from about 1860 depicts.

tated in December 1874 that 'it was ound that the privilege was not availed of to an extent to warrant the company n setting aside so much space in ach train'. Thus female passengers howed by their actions that the extra rotection was not needed, and most ailways, driven by the financial need to ll trains, usually provided 'ladies only' ompartments only 'on request'. They emained rare, and in 1887 a Board of rade report stated that even when they vere requested they were underused.

It did not become widely acceptable for women to smoke until the twentieth century; therefore the smoking compartment was used predominantly by men.

Before 1880 on-board toilets on trains were not a common feature. Only n the South Eastern Railway (SER) between 1848 and 1850 were some arriages introduced with washbasins and chamber pots. In the 1860s some amily saloon carriages were equipped with them, with most sleeping cars cquiring them in the 1870s.

However, being 'caught short' was a recognised problem. A commentator n the 1860s referred to 'Gentlemen who are so delicately nurtured that t makes them uncomfortable to hear that other people are deprived of access o a lavatory for three whole hours'. However, some methods of obtaining elief were found. Ladies travelling together are known to have concealed hamber pots in baskets, while devices for men were advertised whereby ong tubes were strapped to the leg under the trousers.

However, with the introduction of larger carriages in the 1880s irst-class compartments started to be routinely built with en-suite toilets. Nevertheless, only in the 1890s, when corridor coaches, in which bassengers could pass between carriages, were introduced on long-distance ervices, did lavatory facilities become available for all, but toilets emained uncommon on suburban services.

In the railways' formative years, passengers could buy newspapers or books, but little else, to read on their journey. In 1849 Routledge began publishing its 'Railway Library', which was available at stations. The books vere nicknamed 'yellowbacks', after the colour of their binding, and were heaply made. Over fifty years 1,277 titles were produced, including works by Robert Louis Stevenson and Jane Austen.

This label was placed in the window of a compartment to denote that it was for the exclusive use of women.

While these were published throughout the period, periodicals eventually became the most popular form of railway reading. A pioneer publisher was George Newnes, who in October 1881 issued the first edition of *Tit-Bits*. Its editor described its purpose:

It is impossible for any man in the busy times of the present to even glance at any large number of the immense variety of books and papers which have gone on accumulating, until now their number is fabulous. It will be the business of the conductors of *Tit-Bits* to find out from this immense field of literature the best things that have been said or written, and weekly to place them before the public for one penny.

Indeed, it condensed works by authors such as Dickens and Disrael into easily consumable chunks for passengers. Furthermore, it featured anecdotes, stories, competitions, historical pieces, advertisements and readers' correspondence, as well as other miscellaneous articles. Overall it was a new approach to publishing.

After *Tit-Bits*, Newnes founded other periodicals, including *The Strand Magazine* (1891), *The Million* (1892), *The Westminster Gazette* (1893), *Country Life* (1897), *The Wide World Magazine* (1898) and *The Captain* (1899). *The Strand Magazine* contained serialised stories from contributors including H. G. Wells, Agatha Christie, E. Nesbit, Rudyard Kipling, Arthur Morrison, Dorothy L. Sayers and P. G. Wodehouse, and it was here that Arthur Conan Doyle introduced Sherlock Holmes. With these publications Newnes tapped into a burgeoning market – the commuter of the upper lower class and the lower middle class, who after 1870 were an increasingly large proportion of all railway passengers. His success was such that by the mid-1890s *The Strand*'s monthly circulation had reached 500,000.

The Strand Magazine was the most successful of George Newnes's publications and introduced the world to Sherlock Holmes.

Early travellers wishing to read on evening or night-time trains would have been disappointed, because carriage lighting was initially poor. On its opening in 1838, the GWR installed none. At first, most lamps burned rape oil, which provided poor illumination, and a Board of Trade regulation stated that each carriage compartment should have two lamps. However, this was applied variably, and in September 1854 the *Preston Guardian* reported that there was no lighting on evening journeys between Blackpool and Preston.

Improvements were introduced slowly. In May 1857 experiments were made at the Albion Foundry, York, with a 'dry gasometer' fitted on a carriage's underside. This held oal gas that was fed into compartments through tubes to the lamps. Many similar experiments occurred around this time, and in September 1861 a carriage's gas tank exploded at the East Lancashire Railway's Bury works, killing the foreman. This lighting method was costly to install and never widely adopted. Only the North London Railway (in 1862) installed it on all its trains, with a gas tank in the brake van.

In the late 1870s and the 1880s cheaper systems became available that compressed the gas in tanks under the carriage. However, while more companies adopted gas lighting, its installation was still slow, and it did not become dominant until the 1890s. Indeed, in 1891 the LNWR's passenger carriages still used 26,000 oil lamps.

Electricity became available for lighting after 1870, and the first electric lights were used in 1881 on the LBSCR's Pullman

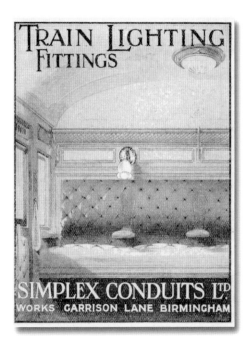

car *Beatrice*. However, like gas, the technology was adopted slowly. The light was poor and yellowish, and the equipment was expensive to fit. Not until J. Stone patented a system in 1894 that charged batteries from dynamos attached to carriage wheels did it become cheaper. Nevertheless, by 1911 a letter to *The Times* suggested that 75–80 per cent of carriages were still gas-lit.

By the First World War numerous companies were designing electric lighting specifically for carriages.

Most travellers throughout the period bought food before starting their journeys, and by 1870 many companies provided the option for passengers to purchase 'luncheon baskets'. In the 1880s the LNWR advertised baskets containing '*Cold Meat* – Beef, or Chicken with Ham or Tongue, and salad, Bread, Butter, Cheese, Ice &c.' for 2s 6d at selected refreshment rooms. Furthermore, 'half a bottle of Claret, two glasses of Sherry, or a bottle of Ale or Stout' cost 6d extra.

Yet around this period the food options for first-class passengers improved. On 1 November 1879 the GNR introduced a Pullman restaurant car, imported from the United States, on its London to Leeds route. The *Liverpool Mercury* stated that

> those who arrived at King's Cross were loud in their praise of the excellent manner in which, while the train was travelling at a very high rate of speed, the midday meal was served and the ease with which they partook of it.

Initially, restaurant cars were reserved for first-class passengers, who were prohibited from changing carriages throughout their journey. However, with the introduction of corridor coaches, this requirement became less common.

Indeed, by the 1890s railways saw the potential of restaurant cars to attract passengers, especially where they were in competition with other companies. Thus, in the 1890s the first third-class restaurant facilities were introduced, and by 1914 they could be found on the long-distance services of most major railway companies.

The first sleeping facilities on Britain's railways were introduced in 1847 when the LBSCR began running first-class saloons with convertible sofas 'for general use and the convenience of invalids'. These were known as 'bed carriages'.

However, not until February 1873 were true 'sleeper' services introduced by the North British Railway (NBR), which put Pullman cars on trains between London King's Cross and Glasgow. These had berths that were converted from seats, and the sleeping arrangements were communal. Unfortunately, the first trial was unsuccessful. The service was very full and on reaching Berwick-upon-Tweed an axlebox was found to be on fire, necessitating the removal of the carriage from the train.

Only in 1890 did the familiar sleeper services appear on the GWR, the carriages having corridors, off which were compartments containing berths. Subsequently, carriages of this format were used on the East and West Coast routes, especially during the 'races' to Scotland, on trains to the West Country, and those between London and northern cities. All the passengers were first-class, paying supplementary fares. Third-class passengers wishing to sleep were always restricted to their seats.

Most of the improvements within passenger carriages occurred after 1870. However, the sleeping and restaurant cars were not very profitable.

This LNWR dining-car train from 1905 was one of the prestige services the company operated.

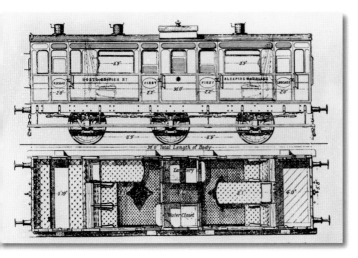

This is a plan
of Britain's first
sleeping carriage,
which ran between
London and
Glasgow in 1873.
Initially a charge of
10s was made, but
this was reduced
to 5s by 1877.

or railway companies. They were heavy, costing more to haul; they held
fewer passengers than standard carriages, diminishing their capacity to
generate revenue; and they were very expensive to build. Thus it has been
argued that, like increased carriage sizes generally, they contributed to
the industry's decreasing profitability in the period.

A third-class
restaurant car
of the Glasgow
& South Western
Railway from 1910.

THE PERILS OF RAILWAY TRAVEL

N August 1868 the *Saturday Review* stated:

> We are, in the matter of railway travelling, always treading the unknown...
> All that we know of the future is that it is full of dangers; but what these
> dangers are we cannot conjecture or anticipate.

These comments came after thirty years in which fear of accidents had increased significantly, and by 1870 public concern was at its height.

Numerous factors created this fear. Firstly, passengers' safety was in the hands of others. In 1874 the *Fortnightly Review* commented:

> Every train from its starting to its destination, goes through a series of the
> most marvellous hairbreadth escapes; and if the travelling public had
> an inkling of the pitfalls that beset them, comparatively few would venture
> from home.

Secondly, the rigid Victorian social structures did not apply regarding accidents, as their victims were from all classes, statuses, occupations and genders. After the 1868 Abergele disaster, the worst in Britain up to then, the *Saturday Review* commented: 'We are all railway travellers; these trains and collisions, these stations and engines, and all the rest of it, are not only household words, but part of our daily life.'

Lastly, surviving accidents was a matter of luck. One individual might be killed, while others would escape physically unharmed. On the GNR at Abbots Ripton in 1876 two trains collided; Lord Colville walked away, while the two people sitting opposite him were killed. Indeed, Tennyson's poem 'Charity' contains the lines:

> Two trains clashed; then and there he was crushed in a moment and died,
> But the new-wedded wife was unharmed, though sitting close at his side.

Opposite:
As the number of railways grew, it became clear that regulation was required to ensure safety on the railways. H. C. Rothery, a wreck commissioner, stated that the Tay Bridge, which collapsed on 28 December 1879, was 'badly designed, badly constructed and badly maintained'. This illustration from *Look and Learn* dramatically depicts the accident.

Yet railway companies were not liable when accidents occurred, the blam[e] for them being placed on the individual employee at fault. Consequentl[y] hostility towards the companies grew, the public viewing them as despot[ic] regimes that put profit before human life through their resistance t[o] investing in costly safety devices. The *Lancet* argued in 1857 that compani[es] maintained through by-laws 'their right to slay, smash, mutilate, or cripp[le]' their unlucky passengers. They utterly ignore all responsibility for th[e] occurrence of these little accidents.'

However, the public's indignation was also aimed at government, whic[h] they perceived as being unwilling to force companies to make safe[ty] improvements. In 1842 the Board of Trade had received authority to investigat[e] accidents. However, it was powerless to impose changes on the compani[es] based on its findings. In 1862 the *Saturday Review* argued that railway accident[s] 'might be more correctly described as pre-arranged homicide', implyin[g] that there was collusion between the railway industry and the governmen[t]. Indeed, this was not an unreasonable perspective, considering that in 186[2] 125 out of 658 members of Parliament were railway company director[s]. Indeed, this group became known as the 'Railway Interest'.

With the railway companies and government seemingly unwilling t[o] improve safety, two private companies played on passengers' fears to mak[e]

Fear of accidents was present from the beginning of the railways, as this 1831 etching by Henry Hughes shows. Exploding boilers were indeed a regular occurrence.

The Pleasures of the Rail-Road. — Showing the Inconvenience of a Blo[w...]

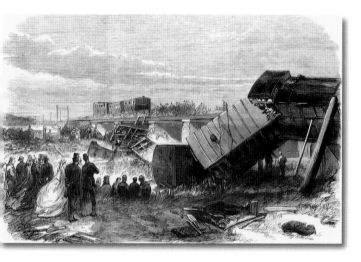

Accidents affected individuals from all levels of Victorian society. This is the 1865 Staplehurst accident, from which Charles Dickens narrowly escaped with his life.

profit. In 1849 the Railway Passengers Assurance Company (RPAC) was formed to sell from station booking offices, with the agreement of the railway companies, accident insurance for train journeys. The price of cover was 3d for first-class journeys, 2d for second and 1d for third. If a fatal accident occurred, the deceased's family would receive £1,000, £500 and £200 respectively. When non-fatal injuries were sustained, the RPAC paid 'a sum of compensation that they consider just'. Monthly insurance tickets could also be purchased, and, irrespective of the class of ticket, fatal accidents would entitle the deceased's family to £1,000. The scheme was immediately successful, and between August 1849 and the third week in February 1850 over 65,000 single-journey tickets were sold.

Consequently, the types of policies on offer were increased. In 1897 insurance could be bought for journeys above or below 35 miles in length. Passengers could also purchase cover for one month, three months, six months, five years, ten years or their entire lives. The level of compensation for injuries was formalised, and different amounts were paid for 'loss of two eyes or limbs', 'total disablement' and 'partial disablement'.

By 1897 the Railway Passengers Assurance Company provided passengers with a range of different insurance policies, as indicated by this guide for stationmasters.

While the RPAC was the main passenger insurer, in May 1885 George Newnes's *Tit-Bits*, on the suggestion of a reader's widow, announced 'A NEW SYSTEM OF LIFE ASSURANCE', as follows:

ONE HUNDRED POUNDS [later increased to £1,000] WILL BE PAID …
TO THE NEXT-OF-KIN OF ANY PERSON WHO IS KILLED IN A
RAILWAY ACCIDENT, PROVIDED A COPY OF THE CURRENT ISSUE
OF *TIT-BITS* IS FOUND UPON THE DECEASED.

The first successful claimants were the family of a forty-year-old coachbuilder who had been killed falling between the train and the platform at Hatfield station. Four witnesses testified that *Tit-Bits* was in his pocket. By September 1891 thirty-six families had received money. Whether the scheme increased *Tit-Bits*' circulation is unknown. However the accidents did provide its readers with gripping stories.

Not all accidents were the companies' fault. George Findlay, the LNWR's general manager, stated in 1889 that fog was the 'one element which causes, perhaps, more anxiety upon those engaged in the management of the railway than all others put together'. Heavy snow was also dangerous causing the accidents at Abbots Ripton in 1876 and Eliot Junction in 1906.

Like the railways, *Tit-Bits* used postcards to promote its insurance scheme.

'TIT-BITS' INSURES YOUR LIFE FOR £1,000.

Nevertheless, most accidents during the period occurred because of the technology or lack of it, employed by the railways, or by signalling errors. Moreover, increasing traffic density on the network also increased the risks, and as early as the 1860s Clapham Junction was handling seven hundred trains per day, Cannon Street was handling 525, and 1,200 passed through London Bridge.

In the 1840s and 1850s accidents were commonly caused because trains were controlled by time interval. Trains would not be started from a station until a specified amount of time had elapsed since the preceding one had departed. Therefore, if a train stopped between stations, for whatever reason, an accident could be prevented only by the guard of the first train going back along the line to provide warning. Unsurprisingly, the system sometimes failed notably causing accidents at Glasgow in 1850 Frodsham in 1856 and Egham in 1864.

In the 1860s the introduction of 'block working' became the recognised response to the problem. Using the electric telegraph, which was introduced on most lines in the 1840s, this system controlled trains by distance intervals. The track was split into sections, and by means of a system of bells in signal boxes that alerted signalmen to the locations of trains, trains were not allowed to enter a 'block section' before the preceding train had exited it. However, because of the high installation cost, companies were slow to introduce the system, and a spate of accidents in the 1860s compelled the Board of Trade to ask all companies to report the extent to which they were using block working. They protested, and the NER completely ignored the request. By 1872 block working was in use on only 42 per cent of Britain's railway network.

After 1870 the public outcry over railway safety compelled the government, through the Board of Trade, to begin to monitor it more closely, notwithstanding the Railway Interest,

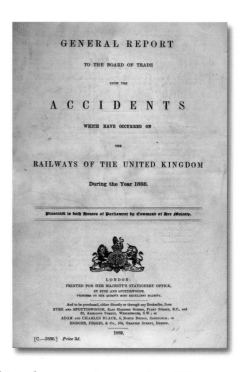

which made Parliament highly reluctant to legislate to force companies to improve safety. The 1842 Regulation of Railways Act had obliged companies to inform the Board of Trade of accidents 'attended with serious personal injury to the public'. However, another act in 1871 extended this to 'any person whatsoever' (including railway employees), and the Board of Trade could establish courts of enquiry to investigate major accidents. A further act in 1873 forced companies to provide returns on the extent of block working in their systems. Also, between 1874 and 1878 there was a Royal Commission on railway safety. However, this produced few results.

The poor braking power of trains also became an issue in the 1870s. Continuous brakes, whereby trains were brought to a halt by the slowing of each vehicle's wheels, were the logical answer, and in 1878 government ordered the companies to provide twice-yearly returns of the number of vehicles on which they were installed. Nevertheless, while some railways began fitting vehicles with devices in the late 1870s and 1880s, they were not forced to, and most used the fact that different braking systems were available to delay commitment to its implementation.

Then, on 12 June 1889, near Armagh in Ireland, a train of Sunday-school children stalled on an incline. To lighten the load, the crew divided the train, and the locomotive pulled the front section forward. They intended

From 1842 the Board of Trade gained the power to investigate all railway accidents in Britain and produced a summary report each year.

The accident at Rednal in June 1865 is not as well-known as that at Staplehurst in the same year. However, thirteen people died and thirty were injured.

to come back for the rear portion. However, lacking continuous brakes it rolled down the gradient and collided with a train behind. Eighty people died, a third of whom were children, and 260 were injured. It was the United Kingdom's worst railway accident to date.

The accident caused an outcry, and the House of Commons requested that the President of the Board of Trade, Michael Hicks-Beach, attend to answer questions. He revealed that only one in six of vehicles in Ireland 18 per cent of passenger carriages in England and 40 per cent in Scotland had continuous brakes. *British Architect* noted that 'the time has come when Parliament may undertake a little legislation on the question'. The 1889 Regulation of Railways Act was speedily passed, forcing the railways to adopt block working, continuous brakes, and interlocking between signals and points.

Before 1889 the railways and government had procrastinated over railway safety. The railways resisted installing known safety devices for cost reasons, while governments dithered because many members of Parliament were railway directors, and, possibly, because they did not want to interfere with the freedom of businesses. Yet the Armagh accident compelled the government, in the face of public pressure, to act, and after the Act of 1889 accident rates fell dramatically. Between 1885 and 1889 there were on average 27.6 passenger deaths and 639.8 injuries per year on Britain's railways. However, these figures dropped to 13.2 deaths and 487.2 injuries between 1895 and 1899. Clearly, earlier action would have saved lives.

TRAVEL FOR WORK AND LEISURE

TRAVELLING FOR WORK

Most passengers in the Victorian period travelled for work purposes. However, the railway companies were initially not interested in serving commuters, as main-line stations were spaced far apart. Indeed, when the London & Birmingham Railway (LBR) opened in 1837 the first station outside Euston was at Harrow, nearly 12 miles away.

It has been suggested that this was because there were few customers close to cities. However, suburban construction costs were also a factor. The LBR's secretary, Richard Creed, stated in 1839: 'there is one expense no engineer could estimate, the expense of stations, and there we have arrived at a fearful excess.' Indeed, the company's line through Camden Town to Euston cost £380,000. Companies, therefore, opted for serving the more profitable long-distance commuters.

Not until the 1840s did railways start serving suburban markets. The LSWR's Wandsworth station (now Clapham Junction) was 2 miles from its Nine Elms terminus; the London & Croydon Railway's New Cross station was 3 miles from London Bridge, as was the London & Greenwich Railway's Deptford station. In the 1840s the LSWR specifically built lines for outer-suburban passengers, such as to Richmond, and the companies also encouraged house building in the districts they served. Later, in the 1850s, railways were built in residential areas, such as the Liverpool, Crosby & Southport Railway and the North London Railway, and more stations were opened nearer the terminals. Consequently between the 1840s and 1860s commuter numbers grew. The London & Blackwall Railway carried 1,460,550 passengers in 1843, but this increased to 3,452,288 in 1844.

Nevertheless, an 1855 government select committee estimated that most workers still came to London by other means. Four hundred thousand walked, eighty thousand used omnibuses, thirty thousand used steamers, and 52,000 took other vehicles. Only 62,440 used Paddington, Euston, King's Cross, Fenchurch Street and London Bridge stations. Indeed, most urban workers could not afford railway travel.

Opened between 1836 and 1838, the London & Greenwich Railway was London's first railway, and could be considered Britain's first commuter line.

Of the 62,000 people who could afford first- or second-class accommodation, such as bankers, clerks and managers, many occasionally travelled in third class for short journeys. Nevertheless, Captain Laws, the Manchester & Leeds Railway's general manager, stated in 1844 that third-class travellers were principally 'the working classes, weavers, masons, bricklayers, carpenters, mechanics and labourers of every description'. This implies that skilled workers used third class and those walking were unskilled labourers.

Before the 1860s the only trains available to unskilled labourers were the 'Parliamentary trains', established by the Regulation of Railways Act of 1844 after the Sonning Cutting accident. These trains had to comprise enclosed carriages, to call at all stations, and to move faster than 12 mph, and tickets were not to cost more than 1d per mile. Reflecting the financial burden on the railway companies, income from the trains was untaxed. However, the companies objected to running the 'Parlies', stating that many 'Parliamentary' passengers could afford better accommodation. Indeed this may have been so, as in their first full year of operation, from June 1845 to June 1846, 10 per cent of Britain's 40 million passenger journeys were made on them.

After the 1860s those travelling to work by train increased significantly as reflected by the number of season tickets issued. In 1860 railway companies issued 47,894, but by 1875 the total was 597,257, and in 189

he number reached 1,537,765. Season tickets were issued mainly to
irst- and second-class travellers, third-class issues being rare. However,
s described, the number of ordinary third-class tickets sold increased
ignificantly after 1870, constituting 91 per cent of the 1.1 million sold
1 1899. A large part of the growth occurred on commuter routes, and the
ireat Eastern's chairman stated that its suburban passengers had increased
1 number from 1.7 million to 12.9 million between 1867 and 1881. Yet the
ost of rail travel was still expensive for many in the 1890s, and the social
roups using the railways for work were similar to those in the 1850s.

In addition to the 'Parlies', unskilled workers from the 1860s could also
ravel on 'workmen's trains'. When railways were being built, large tracts
f urban housing were demolished. Therefore, many acts granting railway
ompanies construction rights compelled them to provide cheap trains
or the dispossessed workmen, who were consequently living further from
1e metropolis. The first company to receive such a stipulation was the
ireat Eastern, and the act allowing it to extend to Liverpool Street in 1864
rdered the running of workmen's trains to London from Edmonton and
Valthamstow for a fare of no more than 2d. Thus, by 1899, 104 'workmen's
ains' were timetabled daily. Unsurprisingly, the companies saw them as

Commuters
waiting at Slough
station on the
GWR in 1907.

The Manchester, Sheffield and Lincolnshire Railway's New Holland Pier station, in North Lincolnshire, was where passengers could transfer to a ferry to cross the Humber estuary to Hull.

The Pier Station, New Holland.

Workmen's trains, despite being run at inconvenient hours, were heavily patronised. This image shows passengers alighting at Victoria Station in 1865.

loss-making and ran them in the early morning and very late at night, t avoid disrupting the regular services.

By the 1870s the 'Parlies' were becoming a contentious issue for th railway industry. The specified 12 mph was by then painfully slow, and mos

xpress trains carried third-class accommodation. In 1890 George Findlay, ne LNWR general manager, stated that 'in 1872 the Parliamentary train om Euston to Liverpool, 201¾ miles, stopped at every station on the route, nd occupied nearly eleven hours on the journey which the more fortunate nird-class passenger of today is enabled to perform in 4½ hours'.

The railways pressured the government for changes, culminating in the 883 Cheap Trains Act. This exempted all tickets costing one penny per mile om duty, irrespective of the trains' speed or stopping frequency, effectively nishing the 'Parly'. However, G. J. Holyoake, who championed their pandonment, praised them in 1901, stating that 'to workmen of small means ne Parliamentary train was a considerable device as it enabled thousands o travel who otherwise could not avel at all'.

In this period excursion trains ere a big part of people's leisure tivities. Either directly or through ntermediaries, groups would nake agreements with railways to onvey them to and from places a reduced price. This gave ustomers economical travel, while uaranteeing income for the ompanies. While the LMR initially n trains for specific occasions, the rst known excursion was put on 1831 when it agreed, through a romoter, to take 150 members of ennett Street Sunday School from iverpool to Manchester and back r one-third of the regular fare.

Excursions soon became more umerous and popular, conveying oups to various events, including ce meetings, church bazaars, or st to visit cities. The *Sheffield & otherham Independent* reported April 1841 that during the /hitsuntide holidays the North idland Railway would operate n excursion train from Sheffield Derby, when no doubt that ousands of our townsmen will

A handbill from 1877 promoting cheap excursion tickets to the Handel Festival of music.

take the opportunity of visiting that pleasant town and its arboretum. The Bodmin & Wadebridge Railway even arranged an excursion to a public execution in 1836. Thomas Cook began his now well-known business by arranging railway excursions, the first of which took 570 Temperance campaigners to a rally at Loughborough in 1841. However, he was only one of many agents who appeared in the 1840s.

With locomotive technology limited and carriages being small, early excursion trains were long. In September 1840 one from Sheffield to Leeds had five locomotives and seventy carriages. Another, arranged by the Leeds Institute in 1840, took 1,250 passengers in a forty-carriage train to Hull. Consequently, excursion trains often arrived so late at their destinations that they had to leave again shortly after, much to the chagrin of the passengers.

The Great Exhibition in Hyde Park between 1 May and 15 October 1851 was an early high point of the excursion train. By this time the railway network was well established, with many London terminals. This allowed excursions to the Exhibition to be arranged from as far afield as Yorkshire and some companies, such as the GNR and the LNWR, engaged in ticket price competition. Overall, all companies running trains to the Exhibition experienced increased traffic, and Thomas Cook claimed that he had brought 165,000 individuals into Euston for it. Consequently, the railways contributed to the Exhibition's success.

After the 1850s excursions became an accepted railway activity, even though some companies questioned their profitability, and massively long

Temperance societies used excursion trains to provide outings for their members. The one pictured, with three steam locomotives, is the 'West Cornwall Teetotal Gala Excursion Train'.

rains disappeared. Excursions were run to major events, such as Manchester rt Exhibition of 1857 and the 1862 International Exhibition in London. urthermore, after the 1871 Bank Holiday Act, which created public holidays n Boxing Day, Easter Monday, Whit Monday and the first Monday in ugust, the numbers of such trains grew significantly.

This was because the railways capitalised on people having more free me and more disposable income, and on the increased popularity of isure activities. Indeed, real wages for most people increased over the ineteenth century, while prices dropped between 1874 and 1896 by 0 per cent. How many people used excursions is uncertain. However, in 865 the Royal Commission on Railways heard that excursions on the ancashire & Yorkshire Railway (LYR), LNWR and Midland Railway carried ,140,000 passengers, constituting three per cent of their passenger evenue. This proportion possibly grew, and between 1901 and 1909 xcursion revenue constituted ten per cent of the LBSCR's passenger come. However, that company predominantly served passenger districts, /hereas the former three did not, so the comparison is poor.

Excursions continued to serve the coast, race meetings, religious atherings, cities, the Boat Race, and fairs run by organisations. Furthermore, om the 1870s the National Sunday League, which was established in 855 to campaign for parks and museums to be opened on Sundays, also egan organising excursions. In 1889 it arranged twenty-two, but by 1914 he number was 540. Large companies, for example the brewers Bass

Passengers could take day trips to places all over the country. Travellers are shown here at Leigh Court station, on the GWR, Somerset, in the 1890s.

Passengers waiting to depart from Box Hill and Burford Bridge station (now Box Hill and Westhumble) on the LB&SCR in the late nineteenth century.

By the First World War promotional handbills had changed little, still heavily relying on text.

in Burton upon Trent, arrange day trips to the seaside fo their workers. The GWR itse arranged an annual 'Swindon Trip taking 26,000 people, over half th town's population, out for th day to resorts such as Weymouth.

Excursion trains also increase the appeal of organised sport particularly cricket and footba Cricket before 1878, whil nationally popular, was only 'local' game. Yet, in that yea the Australian cricket tean visited and railways ran excursic trains to the matches. Buildir on this success, later excursions to cricket matches helped turn the spon into a national game. Similarly, as football's popularity grew in th 1870s, 1880s and 1890s, excursion trains built up teams' fan bases t transporting supporters to matches. In 1872 two thousand people attende the Football Association Cup Final, but by 1901 the figure was 110,00(most of whom came by train.

It was the Victorians who began the tradition of taking week-long holidays. Holiday resorts for richer people, who before then were the only ones taking such breaks, developed as soon as the railways reached the sea. While initially many main-line railways ignored this traffic, smaller companies fostered it. By 1837 thousands went to the coast each summer, particularly in Scotland. In 1840, for example, the Preston & Wyre Railway opened a line to the new port at Fleetwood, which offered summer bathing. Later, main-line companies serving the south coast, such as the LSWR, LCDR and LBSCR, immediately saw the profit of appealing to holidaymakers. *The Standard* reported in 1844 that 'three of the railways that are now running holiday trains, viz., the Dover, the Brighton, and the Southampton lines, present peculiar inducements to holiday folk...'

By the 1840s lines were being built to specific resorts, and between 1845 and 1849 fourteen branches of this nature were constructed nationwide, the Bristol & Exeter Railway's Weston-super-Mare line being one example. Companies contributed financially to new resorts, such as those at Barry and Silloth, in an attempt to increase profits. When connected to the railway network, spa towns such as Bath and Leamington Spa also became popular holiday destinations.

Before the 1860s only the wealthier portions of society took holidays, but this started to change, and in 1875 a Civil Service enquiry commission found that fortnight-long holidays were allowed to most clerical and administrative employees, and those who were long-serving or in higher grades may even have received three or four weeks' leave, some with pay. Manual workers began to have paid leave in the 1880s, and it was pay, not time, that was decisive in allowing them the opportunity to take holidays. Moreover, increasing numbers of the working class had more disposable income to spend.

Therefore the number of people taking annual holidays grew, a fact the railways capitalised on. After 1870 they offered cheap tickets to anglers, golfers, cyclists and walkers. Cycling became particularly popular, and reduced rates were offered to cyclists through combined tourist tickets'. Indeed, sixty thousand cycles were dispatched from London Bridge station in the summer

'Mrs Smith (to Mr Smith who, starting for his annual "rest cure", is making a frantic rush for the train), "John! Are you *Sure* you locked up the house?"'

of 1898. Furthermore, between 1905 and 1914 the GWR put on train specially for ramblers to places east of Swindon. By 1914 Britain's railway served around two hundred beach resorts, many of which had grown up after 1870 in response to demand. The social researcher Charles Booth stated in 1902 that among all London's classes 'holiday-making was one of the most remarkable changes in habits over the last ten years'.

Naturally marketing was a part of attracting custom. Initially, railways simply advertised in the press to notify travellers of fares, train times or new lines, and produced posters and handbills promoting special fares, excursions and events. However, at first this material was usually in black and white with bold lettering, and not colourful. Only after 1870, with the introduction of chromolithographic printing, did posters become multicoloured and illustrated.

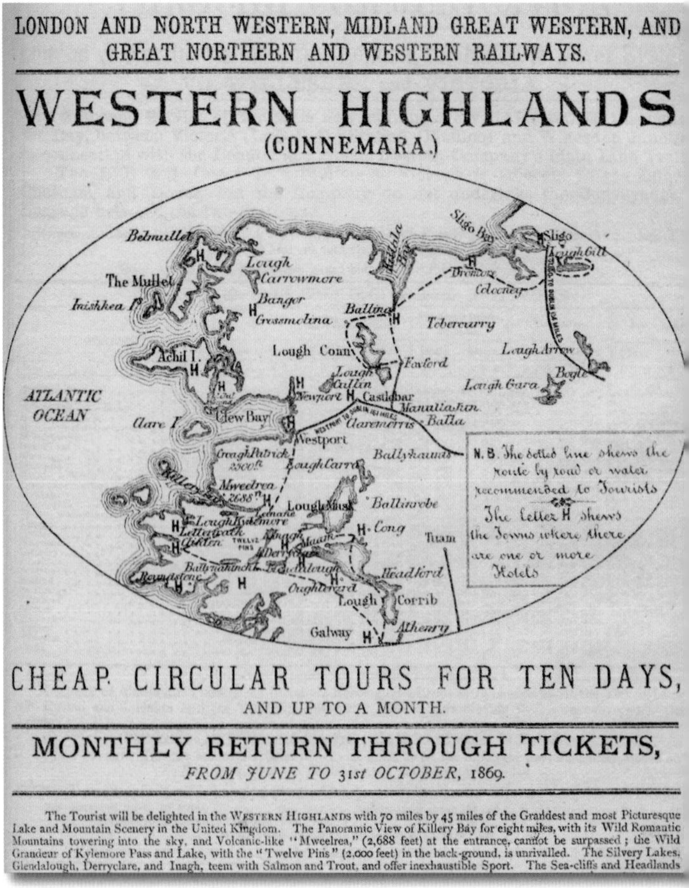

Advertising was basic in the 1860s, with little flamboyance. This advertisement from an LNWR timetable from 1869 delivers a large amount of detail about the company's holiday tickets, which continues over many lines beyond those shown here.

Guidebooks to the territory the railways served were available throughout. These were initially published independently and contained information on interesting features along companies' lines, as well operational and technical details. The first was the *Railway Companion, by a Tourist*, from 1833, which contained illustrated text describing the Liverpool & Manchester's route. As more lines opened, the market for these books increased. Between 1852 and 1866 George Measom printed guides to nine British main lines and two Irish ones, and Bradshaw started producing his *Handbook* from 1863.

The sets of postcards sold by railway companies at stations usually came in envelopes such as this.

Between the 1880s and the First World War railway advertising became more sophisticated and was aimed at particular types of customer.

After 1870 the railways themselves also started publishing guides that contained no operational details but described the history and landscapes along their routes. The LSWR's 1894 guide stated that it would 'prove an entertaining travelling companion and useful supplement to the *London and South Western Timetables*.'

After 1900 railway advertising expanded further and some companies set up dedicated publicity departments. Thus, companies' promotional output increased in volume and quality. The LNWR commissioned Norman Wilkinson to paint high-quality posters, and Frank Pick began the long tradition of London Underground posters in 1908. Furthermore, companies installed vending machines selling postcards depicting their resorts, rolling stock, steamships and the districts they served, and the LNWR reputedly sold eleven million before 1911. The quality of guidebooks improved, and particularly noteworthy was the GWR's *Holiday Haunts*, which from 1904 featured

This Midland
Railway postcard
features an image
of Haddon Hall in
Derbyshire, which
the company
served.

The first edition
of the GWR's
highly successful
Holiday Haunts.

information about resorts and accommodation along its line. By 1914, 100,000 copies had been sold.

Another way almost all railways promoted themselves was through the publication of maps. These usually highlighted the publishing company's network by portraying its own lines boldly, while those of competitors were often distorted or omitted. Furthermore, these maps were commonly adorned with advertisements drawing attention to the services the company provided, or images of the regions they served. Only those maps provided in 'general' guides, such as *Bradshaw*, could be relied on for a correct representation of all companies' lines and geographical coverage.

Station hotels for weary travellers were an early development. The first was built by Lord Crewe beside Crewe station in 1837. Railway companies soon built their own, and the London & Birmingham Railway built twin hotels at Euston in 1839. Thereafter other companies leased or purchased hotels, and in 1900 all London termini, except Waterloo, Fenchurch Street and Blackfriars, had one. By 1913 railway companies owned 112 hotels nationally.

The London Bridge
station hotel was
one of the best in
the country when
opened in 1861.

A map of the
Metropolitan
District Railway's
system in 1888.

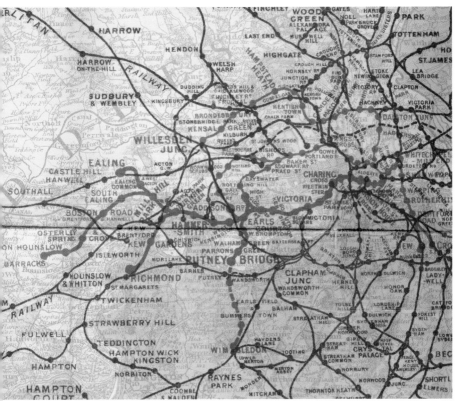

Unsurprisingly, only wealthier people could afford to stay in these hotels. On leasing the Southampton Imperial Hotel in 1866, the LSWR's directors stated that 'a first class hotel will be obtained which will be conducive to the comfort of the passengers to and from Southampton, as well as advantage to this company'. Thus, because of these high standards in 1905 five of London's eleven station hotels were awarded five stars by Baedeker. Yet they were rarely profitable: their purpose was not profit but to feed the company with traffic. In 1913 the expenses of the hotel at Paddington station exceeded income by 35 per cent.

Changes in who travelled by train occurred in the 1870s and 1880s. Before this time a small proportion of society travelled by train for work and leisure, and holidays were the preserve of the elite. Indeed, with fewer passengers to appeal to, promotional material was basic. Later, with more people having greater free time and increased disposable income, more employees travelled for work and pleasure. The railway companies capitalised on this by expanding services, putting on more third-class accommodation and producing promotional material. It was between 1870 and 1914 that the idea of a halcyon age of holiday railway travel began to develop.

Some railways produced elaborate publicity material for their hotels. This is a tariff guide for all the LNWR hotels in the mid-1880s.

CONCLUSION

THIS BOOK has explored many facets of Victorian railway travel from stations and carriages through to destinations and pastimes. It has shown that changes occurred from the 1870s that transformed experience of travelling on the railways. Between 1830 and the 1860s railway travel was slow, austere, available to only a small number of people, functional, and unnerving. However, changes thereafter meant that by 1900 it was comfortable, within the financial reach of most, relatively quick, used for all activities, and very safe. Consequently, the improvements that the railways made to passenger's travelling experiences after 1870, which at different times were driven by the companies themselves, passenger pressure or through the government changing the law, created the basis for how we experience railway travel today.

However, it should also be recognised that these improvements were part of the broader process of the British railway industry becoming progressively mature. Before 1870, the railways' development was relatively slow compared with the dramatic changes that came after that date. From 1870 the technology the railways employed became highly refined, operating procedures became standardised, management practices became systemised and less *ad hoc*, and the career railway employee developed. Thus, most problems of the industry's formative years, when there was much more trial and error in all aspects of railway work, were gradually eliminated in the last part of the century.

The Liverpool terminus of the Liverpool & Manchester Railway in 1833.

Therefore, the enhancements to railway travel introduced after 1870, such as improved safety measures, better quality carriages, faster trains, enhanced station facilities and dining cars, were only elements in the general development in the period toward a railway industry that by the First World War resembled the one which we use directly or indirectly today.

FURTHER READING

Acworth, W. M. *Railways of England*. 1900.

Aldcroft, D., and Freeman, M. (editors). *Transport in the Industrial Revolution*. Manchester University Press, 1983.

Bagwell, P. S. *The Transport Revolution from 1770*. Batsford, 1974.

Bradshaw, G. *Bradshaw's Descriptive Railway Hand-book of Great Britain and Ireland*. 1863; reprinted Old House, 2010.

Dyos, H. J., and Aldcroft, D. H. *British Transport*. Leicester University Press, 1979.

Foxwell, E., and Farrar, T. C. *Express Trains English and Foreign*. 1889.

Head, F. *Stokers and Pokers*. 1894; reprinted David & Charles, 1968.

Jackson, A. A. *London's Termini*. David & Charles, 1978.

Kellett, J. R. *Railways and Victorian Cities*. Routledge & Kegan Paul, 1979.

Kichenside, G. *The Restaurant Car*. David & Charles, 1979.

Leipmann, K. *The Journey to Work*. Kegan Paul, 1944.

Peacock, T. B. *Great Western Suburban Services*. Halstead, 1948.

Perkin, Harold. *The Age of the Railway*. David & Charles, 1971.

Richards, Jeffrey, and MacKenzie, John. *The Railway Station: A Social History*. Oxford University Press, 1988.

Robbins, M. *The Railway Age*. Penguin, 1965.

Schivelbusch, W. *The Railway Journey: Trains and Travel in the Nineteenth Century*. Basil Blackwell, 1980.

Simmons, Jack. *The Railway in Town and Country 1830–1914*. David & Charles, 1986.

Simmons, Jack. *The Victorian Railway*. Thames & Hudson, 1991.

Smith, David Norman. *The Railway and Its Passengers: A Social History*. David & Charles, 1988.

Wilson, R. B. *Go Great Western: A History of GWR Publicity*. David & Charles, 1970.

PLACES TO VISIT

Buckinghamshire Railway Centre, Quainton Road Station, Quainton, Nr Aylesbury HP22 4BY. Telephone: 01296 655720.
Website: www.bucksrailcentre.org

Dartmouth Steam Railway, Queens Park Station, Torbay Road, Paignton TQ4 6AF. Telephone: 01803 555872.
Website: www.dartmouthrailriver.co.uk

Didcot Railway Centre, Didcot Parkway, Didcot, Oxfordshire OX11 7NJ. Telephone: 01235 817200. Website: www.didcotrailwaycentre.org.uk

East Somerset Railway, Cranmore Railway Station, Cranmore, Shepton
   Mallet, Somerset BA4 4QP. Telephone: 01749 880417.
   Website: www.eastsomersetrailway.com

Embsay & Bolton Abbey Steam Railway, Bolton Abbey Station, Bolton Abbey,
   Skipton, North Yorkshire BD23 6AF. Telephone: 01756 710614.
   Website: www.embsayboltonabbeyrailway.org.uk

Great Central Railway, Great Central Station, Great Central Road,
   Loughborough, Leicestershire LE11 1RW. Telephone: 01509 632323.
   Website: www.gcrailway.co.uk

Isle of Wight Steam Railway, The Railway Station, Havenstreet, Isle of Wight
   PO33 4DS. Telephone: 01983 882204.
   Website: www.iwsteamrailway.co.uk

Keighley & Worth Valley Railway, The Railway Station, Haworth, West
   Yorkshire BD22 8NJ. Telephone: 01535 645214.
   Website: www.kwvr.co.uk

Kent & East Sussex Railway, Tenterden Town Station, Station Road,
   Tenterden, Kent, TN30 6HE. Telephone: 01580 765155.
   Website: www.kesr.org.uk

Lakeside & Haverthwaite Railway, Haverthwaite Station, Nr Ulverston,
   Cumbria LA12 8AL. Telephone: 01539 531594.
   Website: www.lakesiderailway.co.uk

Launceston Steam Railway, St Thomas Road, Launceston, Cornwall PL15
   8DA. Telephone: 01566 775665. Website: www.launcestonsr.co.uk

National Railway Museum, Leeman Road, York YO26 4XJ.
   Telephone: 08448 153139. Wesbite: www.nrm.org.uk

North Norfolk Railway, Sheringham Station, Sheringham, Norfolk NR26
   8RA. Telephone: 01263 820 800. Website: www.nnrailway.co.uk

North Yorkshire Moors Railway, 12 Park Street, Pickering, North Yorkshire
   YO18 7AJ. Telephone: 01751 472508. Website: www.nymr.co.uk

Severn Valley Railway, The Railway Station, Bewdley, Worcestershire DY12
   1BG. Telephone: 01299 403816. Wesbite: www.svr.co.uk

South Devon Railway, The Sation, Buckfastleigh, Devon TQ11 0DZ.
   Telephone: 0843 357 1420. Website: www.southdevonrailway.co.uk

STEAM Museum of the Great Western Railway, Kemble Drive, Swindon, SN2
   2TA. Telephone: 01793 466637. Website: www.steam-museum.org.uk

Swanage Railway, Station House, Swanage, Dorset BH19 1HB.
   Telephone: 01929 425800. Website: www.swanagerailway.co.uk

Talyllyn Railway Company, Wharf Station, Tywyn, Gwynedd LL36 9EY.
   Telephone: 01654 710472. Website: www.talyllyn.co.uk

West Somerset Railway, The Railway Station, Minehead, Somerset TA24 5BG.
   Telephone: 01643 704996. Website: www.west-somerset.co.uk

INDEX

Page numbers in italics refer to illustrations